THE END OF THE
HORIZON

BEVERLY SANTIAGO

WestBow
P R E S S

WestBow Press books may be ordered through booksellers or by contacting:

WestBow Press
A Division of Thomas Nelson
1663 Liberty Drive
Bloomington, IN 47403
www.westbowpress.com
1-(866) 928-1240

Because of the dynamic nature of the Internet, any Web addresses or links contained in this book may have changed since publication and may no longer be valid. The views expressed in this work are solely those of the author and do not necessarily reflect the views of the publisher, and the publisher hereby disclaims any responsibility for them.

ISBN: 978-1-4497-0335-6 (sc)
ISBN: 978-1-4497-0336-3 (e)

Library of Congress Control Number: 2010931015

Printed in the United States of America

WestBow Press rev. date: 6/21/2010

Contents

CHAPTER 1
THE BEGINNING!!

Oh, just wondering how I felt by seeing you when you left me by myself and saw all the things you have done. One of the things you must thing is,what are you talking About? Because I'm all confuse and mixed up I rather lay and go to sleep and go and have a sweet dream. But what you are about to read it isn't just a book it is more than a book it is full of adventures and wonderful things that you never seen before. You will thank me by writing this Mystery Book. The story all started like this, I was going to the library and there will always be a guy beside this book shelves and I wonder why. So I tried to get the book behind him but it didn't work out pretty good cause I was in a big trouble.

"What are you doing always standing beside that book, Is there like a secret thing that I can't see or Hear about it?" I asked the guy standing in front of the book.

"Well, I think you are in the wrong place to ask if you really want to know why ask me at 3:30 P.M. cause I am working know!!" said the guy. Well, I was interested so I waited 3 hours just to know why.

Three hours has passed......

"Ok, then here I am, what is the big deal about this book and Why are you standing in front of it?" I said confused.

"There is something wonderful about this book"-The guy grabbing the book at the same time he was talking to me- "No, one has read it only those who really love to read and find themselves missing for their rest of their life."

"What do you mean?" I was really confused and I never heard such of thing like that.

"If you start to read you'll end up in a world you don't know!!" THe guy I knew was trying to explain it, but I don't think this guy is really telling the truth so I was going to get the book and check it out so I could read it and find out if it was truth.

"Give me the book, I want to read it." I said but before I took the book out of his hands He said, "Be careful before you make a wrong decision, cause you then will be an danger!!", "Ok, I will, thank you. Know can I have the book now!!"

"Here take it it will be yours and yours till you find the way to the Horizon, remember before reading the book make a good decision before you start reading this book. And you'll be passing by lava, by forest, by creatures that you don't even know and by decisions you make." That guy scared the crap out of me but that was good that I really didn't care. What happens if he is really telling the truth and that I have to watch for myself, I thought this to myself. I was totally scared. Let's see what happens next. Should I read it or not, this others words I thought to myself when I got home. I can't wait.

Chapter 2
The Starting Point!!

I was walking home still thinking of the book, should I read it today or tomorrow-I thought to myself while walking to my house. I knocked on the door, because the door was closed. The door opened and right there was my friend waiting for me to go to the movies.

"I will read it tomorrow, then!!" I said out loud.

"What did you say?" My friend asked me.

"Oh, nothing." I went inside and change, I couldn't remember that I was going to the movies tonight. I couldn't wait to go to the movie theater, I was going to see the movie called "Facing the Giants." I went downstairs and said, "I'm ready, Sarah. Come on!?!?", "Ok, I was just talking to your mom, Sorry. Hey aren't you in Basketball?"

"Yeah, but instead I went to the Library to check out a book and I found..."

"What did you found in the library?", "Oh, never mind. Lets go to the movie theater and see the movie "Facing the Giants." "Ok, then lets go."

"See-ya mom I am going to live know!!" . "See-ya honey!!"

Walking out of the house we saw a guy standing beside the tree and staring at us. "Let's pray before going to the movies, Okay!!", "Yeah, sure?!?!"

I started praying like this, "God please protect us to our way to the movie theater and that you'll explain us through the movie what to do and what not to do. Please, God give me power to sent away the spirits and that everything that we do it will be good before you. Amen....", "Amen!!"

My others friend's mom picked us up, like about 5 minutes. We got on the car and said to our friend's mom "Hi!" and she said, "Hi!" back. It felt like it been for ever to get to the movie theater, because no one was talking. It felt that you were by yourself.

We got off the car and went through the Movie theater's doors and we were so happy and couldn't wait to see the movie. Everyone said that it was a good movie, because it is a spiritual, and I love spiritual movies. We went in bought some tickets and after that we bought some popcorn, icee, candies, and some hotdogs to eat, too. I couldn't wait till the movie starts. I was so happy. We got the front row to sit on and I felt like me being in the movie. What's next singing in front of the people or what? I was so never when the lady couldn't have a baby but you have to believe in him and everything could happen, even if you are an itheist or a satin-nest you will get a chance to meet God. I guarantee it. The foot ball team was winning I couldn't believe it but it was truth. The coach was telling them that without God you wouldn't be here, because he would just have made the earth without people like when the Dinosaurs existed.

Who would have done us? Scientifically or God. I believe in God. How about you?

CHAPTER 3
THE TIME HAS COME!!

I waked up and saw the book just in front of me. I was thinking to read it, but something came up to my mind and said "Don't do it. Not jet. You are not ready wait for a few days...." but I couldn't wait that long so I grabbed the book and opened it up. I felt a breeze, but it wasn't any kind of breeze it was the weirdest breeze you will ever feel. I started reading and then a few seconds I was right there where a man was standing beside the tree which I saw in front of my house. I was in the desert all around me was covered with sand. Where am I?, I thought to myself. But before I could have thought the guy was walking toward me, Do you want to know what I did? I stood frozen and I knew that this was just a dream. So I started pitching myself but I started to cry, because it really hurt and I knew that this time I wasn't sleeping.

The guy looked like Egyptian and I knew that he would be nice, but all of the sudden I got dizzy and I felt to the ground. All I saw was darkness in my eyes.

"Hallo, vågn op, vågn op. Vågn op, du søvnig hovedet!!" said the guy , trying to wake me up. I opened my eyes and

I saw furniture and ancient stuff, that I never seen. I said, "Hi, you were the guy in front of my house. Right?"

"Hvad siger du jeg kan ikke forstå dig!" the guy said.

"What did you say?" I tried to understand but it was too hard for me.

"Hvad siger du jeg kan ikke forstå dig!" the guy said again. This is going to be a hard time for me to understand. I was so worried if I spoiled something and got in trouble by him. The guy left he didn't really take that much long it been 30 minutes that he hasn't came back. But when he cae back he came with a white man.

"Kan du fortælle hende, at jeg ikke taler Español! Please?" the guy said to the white guy.

"sikker! The guy said that he doesn't talk English and that he was telling you in the beginning to wake up, but you talked like me and he couldn't understand you!"

"Thank God you talk English, Oh I said that too, that I couldn't understand him: >" I said with happiness and sadness.

"Hun sagde, at hun ikke kunne forstå, at du hverken." the white guy said.

"Okay så tak for at oversætte, hvad hun siger, kender jeg til at sove." The went to his little rectangle place that it seem that he was going to sleep.

"He said that he is going to sleep if you want you can come with me or you can stay and go to sleep a little, because it is early."

"Okay then!!" I said tiredly. I went to sleep.

CHAPTER 4
THE AWAKEN ONE...

I waked up and I was so happy that I was not so tired. I stood up and went outside and saw the guy who talked English so I went to him, because I was bored and I didn't know how to live in a world that I didn't really know.

"Oh, so happy that I still am alive." I thought out loud.

"You could say that again I started reading this book at home and so I haven't seen my parents for 7 years, just because a book that I had read."

"So you are telling me that you read a book that took you here?" I said horrified.

"Yes, I didn't do what the librarian said, and here I am stuck in a book that I thought that was just a normal book."

"Well, at least I am here just thinking how am I going to awaken from this dream."

"I wish that so much, any way how old are you?" He said staring at me with those beautiful blue eyes.

"I am 17 years old next year I was going to pass from 12th grade, but I think the that is not going to happen. So how old are you?"

"Well, I am 18 years old, and I missed been in school for 7 years."

"What you were in 5th grade when you read this book?"

"Yeah, I know that was a long time ago."

"I feel sorry, for you :<" , "Why?" , "Because you haven't seen your parents and your family. Doesn't that make you sad and worried?

"Yeah, but that was when I first time I was here I got used to it. I don't know how am I going to get back, but I think it will be pretty soon. I wish."

"Well, at least I'm here." , "What do you mean?" , "That I love you."

"Well, that is not bad, I love you, too. Thanks for saying that because I felt unloved and now I feel loved, thanks from you."

"You welcome." I said with that happiness. Why did I said that in the first place, is it because he looked cute, or is it because he was so nice to me and he was so alone-I thought-what could it be.

We hold hands, but I wasn't taking this as a boyfriend or girlfriend, I was taking this as friends that we were together for along time. What could it be? I thought to myself. After talking to him we went to the tent and ate fresh deer meat.

"How did you guys get this meat if you live in the desert, and plus deers live in the woods, forest, and other places, too?" I said surprised.

"There is this guy who comes from the woods and plus that he know that there is people that lived in the woods, so he comes to the woods sailing meat. It is pretty awesome."

"Oh, well do you know any one who lives in a city?"

"No, in this time of years everyone lives in tents and apart from everyone and there is no cities, they are called villages." , "Oh that is cool"

Me and the guy went outside and got a bow, he was showing me how to shoot a bow and that was cool. To be honest this was my first time shooting a bow and I made it after trying 100 times!! After that we rode the camels and he plus showed me how to ride the camels. I was so happy not only it was awesome it was an adventure and I was so happy. Here I go again I was so happy. The first time riding on the camel I fell down and he was starting laughing at me, but at the same time I was laughing, too. He showed me how to get my balance and get the trick of it. I tried it, but still it didn't work. This is going to be along day, I could feel it.

"Okay do want to go and swim?"

"First what is your name before I keep hanging out with you?"

"My name is Alex, and what is yours?"

"Mine is Sarah, nice to meet you!"

"You have meat me already, so do you want to go swimming?"

"How are we supposed to swim if we live in the dessert."

"There is a river passing by this Dessert place, how you called it."

"Okay then let's go." We went to the river it took 30 minutes to get to the river. When we got there Alex took of his T-shirt and well I took off my long pants, but don't worry I had shorts under them. That was safe. Splash, splash, splash, the water splashed. We played shark and south pole. It was awesome. After a couple of hours we got tired so we went back to the tent. That guy that didn't know how to talk English was just smiling to us. It was night time so I said to Alex goodnight.

Chapter 5

Wake up!!

I had the sweetest dream ever, I was with Alex and we were playing the instrument, and then all of the sudden we were walking into a beautiful place. There was trees on the side and then we end up in a pond swimming and laughing. I was so happy, that I wanted to cry. I don't really know why I wanted to cry, but Alex was hugging me, and I felt this warm breeze around me.

"Wake up, wake up!!" He said. "Wake up!!!!!!" I waked up and I just noticed that it was just a dream.

"Are you okay?" , "Yes, I just had the beautiful and the sweetest dream."

"What was it about, Sarah." , "Oh nothing much.... I mean it was awesome and the sweetest dream ever. It was about you and me."

"Cool, what did we do together."

"We were playing the instrument and then all of the sudden we were walking and we were holding hands.... After holding hands we end up in a pond we were playing and after in the water you hugged me and I felt the warm breeze from your arm. Then I heard someone calling "Wake up wake up" so I ignored that voice, but at the second time I heard "Wake up!!!!" so this time I did what I heard, but then I was confused and so when I waked up I saw you." , "Wow, I don't really know what it means, but we have to deal with it and there is something for us in the Future!!!!"

Chapter 6
The trial!!

We went to this trail it was a weird trail. First, like the old time you have to ride a camel to pass through the desert. Second, we saw different animals that I never seen before, and third we were having so much fun.

The trail was long, plus it was all sand trail. I saw a lizard on the sand and I picked it up, but before the lizard could have bit me, my friend Alex screamed, "Don't touch that, and don't move!!!"

"Why?" , "Just don't move, it will bit you to death.!!" , "Okay, I will do what you say."

It took a long time to get that lizard out of me. He took a big stick out of the dry tree, it broke really easily. He came beside me and stick out the stick toward me. The lizard really fast grab on the stick. Then Alex threw it toward the dry tree and the lizard died.

"That scared me I owe you two now, thanks!!" I said with relieves.

"That is okay you didn't really know about this or did you?" , "No, not really. Why?" , "Just, wondering....?"

We got on the camels and started riding. On our way I started getting dizzy, it was because the sun was harsh on me. ALex stopped by a well and grabbed some water and putted on my forehead.

"Do you feel better. now?"

"Yeah, I feel better,it feels like you are my dad and that you are taking care of me. Why do you think I feel like this, Alex?", "Because I love u."

Chapter 7

What's up!!!

During the trail I heard a lot of voices and I was excited, but when we went on we saw an army fighting against the other army.

"Oh, no I didn't know this will happen, let hide."

We hid be hind the camels, we put on the camel a blanket that was the same color of the sand.

"That will hid us." , "Why are we hiding for?" , "They are all looking for me." , "Why are they looking for you?" , "They think I'm a god, but are you christian?" , "Yeah, why?" , "Well, I don't want to be their god and because I believe in the God that is in heaven, I don't want to do something stupid, like give me this give me that. I don't want to be a god."

"Why won't you stop the army and say that you don't want to be a god?" , "Because they know already, and if I stop the army they will kill me because I didn't want to be their god."

"Well, that is okay. You make your decision I don't make them for you. If that is what God wants you to do well, do what he says."

"Thanks for understanding, you are a pleasant lady."

"You welcome!!!!" When the war was over we stopped hiding and went outside to see what had just happened. There were dead people lying on the floor and their was another one trying to get up and still fight for their country or village. I started crying for what had just happened, but Alex hugged me and said, "Don't cry for they just wanted a God, instead, of crying pray so that others could forgive for what they have done."

I knew that what they did was wrong, but the only thing it was that they didn't have a chance to know about God, and I was sad about that. I have to go on, and forget of what just had happened.

"Let's go." said Alex. "Okay, let's go." I answered back.

We went on the same trail and we kept seen a lot of armies and fighting but each time I saw this I said in my mind, "Forgive them God, because they don't know what they are doing."

We figured out that there was a well on our way, for the help of a little kid who was playing with its old styled toys. A few minutes later we found it, it had a lot of water in it and it was fresh too, because it was beneath a fresh tree, and because the tree was covering the well that had water in it, it was a blessing.

"How does it taste, Sarah?" , "It taste like water" I said joking. "Ah, ah, ah ah,!!" Alex and I were laughing out loud, I usually make the jokes at school, but now there is another person that could handle the jokes as well as I can. I was happy, because if it wasn't for that book I wouldn't be here. It was getting dark so I went around to find some dry sticks and I found a few and put them into a pile so we can make fire. I helped Alex put up the tent and we went hunting for some lizards or what ever that a desert might have. We ate and after that we played music. It was awesome, but know I waited for the next day.

Chapter 8
What's wrong???

It was morning time and I waked up first and then woke up ALex. We were all red, because of the sunburn. It was no fun, but at least we saw a river so we played in the water. Any way where are we going, I thought. If we are traveling so far....why, I kept on thinking these words in my mind. The Alex noticed that I was thinking a lot, I don't really know how he knew that I was thinking, because he came up to me and said, "Are you okay? Because I see you thinkable, if you need to talk to me then talk, I am all open."

"I'm really confused, because we are traveling so far away, but why are we?" , "To get away of the storm and I want to take you some place safe, then been in the dangerous place. You know that guy back where he found you?" , "Yeah, what?", "Well, he is not to controllable to hang out he likes women and he has more than 5 wives, and I wanted to protect you from him. He is from the back then, so back then people are too, sexual."

"Thank you for telling me, Thank you a lot." , "You welcome, do you want to go know?"

"Yeah, I will like to. Do you know when are we going back to our normal lives?" , "I don't really know, but I want it to be pretty soon, because living in this old ways it is too hard to live with. Plus, I'm used to it, I don't really have problems, but I want to see my family already. How about you?" , "Yeah, I do, I miss my family, too." So they both went on.

CHAPTER 9

SNOW???

We were on our way then we figured out that it was getting too cold to be in the dessert. So we put our old style clothes and went on. A few minutes later we saw white stuff coming down from the sky, we acted as we never seen this such of thing, but then when it landed on my nose I said, "It's snow, it's snow!!" , "Oh, no, this doesn't sound good." , "What was wrong?" , "We better hurry up before something horrible happens."

"What is the bad thing haven't you ever seen snow before, or if it's not snow what is it?"

"This isn't those ordinary snow this is the storm I'm talking about, I think it changed directions. We better not look back, you understand me or you'll be scared. I did it ones and I was frighten. You better not look back, You understand me?"

"Yes, I won't look back." But I didn't do what he told me and the camels were running. They felt frighten like I was too. I looked back and there was a wolf following us.

"Aaahh!!" , "I told you to not look back, I told you. Why didn't you do for what I have said?" , "Because I wanted to see what was it." , "Next time don't see the wolf again, because then he will come with 7 more stronger wolves. You wouldn't like to live in prison for your rest of you life, or do you?" , "I'm so sorry will you forgive me?" , "Yes, I forgive you."

Chapter 10

Scared!!!

"I'm scared, I'm scared, Alex!!" , "Don't be scared here I have a note that I wanted to give you if you are going to be with me. Read it."

I read it and it says:

Here you are beside me don't be scared cause God is with you, like God is with me. Don't cry cause you will make me cry too, and say hi cause you never know when I'm not with you. But if I'm gone my spirit is with you and God Holy Spirit will be always with you where ever you go. I love you as a friend, as a dad, as a someone that you never meet before. I love you and this is all I could say. So don't worry, because will always will take care of you even if I'm not beside you.

Sincerely,
Alex

P.S. who Loves you a lot.

"That is so sweet, Thank you. It will be the same with you."

I started crying, because no one has ever wrote a note like that before and I wish I could write those same words to those who I love.

"That will be yours, for your rest of your life, Sarah." Alex said hugging me and talking at the same time. I could be honest with you he is the best guy I ever meet in my life. One day you will have the same feelings.

Chapter 11

What are you doing??

We were this time walking and at the same time we were holding the camels with a rope. We were still in the desert, I was bored seeing the same thing al over, and over again. It was the same thing as if you were eating corn and corn and corn. That is kind of gross.

"What's wrong?" asked Alex.

"I'm getting sick... but really sick." , "Are you getting desert sick?"

"I don't know if it is desert sick, and I haven't even ever heard of desert sick. What is it?"

"It's when you start puking. And turn blue..."

I started puking just before he even said "puking". I puked blue and felt frozen. When I saw my fingers I was worried,

"Don't worry, I know what will do. I have to get Malgamasium." He said looking at me straight in the eye.

"It's is only 15 minutes away. You have to hold your breath or air. So you won't explode."

Explode, I thought, I don't want to explode. Please God help me, help me, help me!!!! I thought I started crying.

23

"You know what with faith I can heal you. Do you have faith?"

"Yes, yes, yes, I do." I said grumpy. I wasn't grumpy but my voice sound like it.

"Let's pray.....hold my hand."

When I hold his hand I felt like the spirit of God was around me like a blanket covering me.

"Before, you pray, I want to tell you. I love you, I love you, love you, love you." Then I felt asleep and I felt peaceful.

"Don't leave me. I love you till the mountains fall down. I love you. Don't leave me." I heard Alex talking to me when I just got up. It was 3:00 A.M. in the morning.

"Alex don't cry I had woken in peace. God had heard you begging him, and I heard you say, "Don't leave me." When I heard you say those words I knew that God was going to respond to your prayer and know I am healed.....I love you too much that when I even say it I know that you are going to love me, too.

Then me and him started crying and we hug each other. This was sad for me and I knew that God healed me. Thank you God all mighty, I know that you had respond his prayers and I thank you for that. Know that I am healed I can have my future how you want me to, I thought this words to myself and when I looked into his eyes he knew that I was talking to God and that I was thanking God for what he had done.

"I felt that I was going to die if you died. I wouldn't survive if you were gone. You make everything so natural and that every time we are together I feel happiness inside me." He said still crying.

"I know,...I know I felt the same way it happened. But know we are suppose to be happy know, because God had healed me. Thank you God(I was saying this part to God.)

Let's have a celebration and thank God for what he had just done."

"Yeah, let's....... Let's have a thank you celebration to God." He said to happiness.

We both hold hands and gave a celebration to God in the desert. Crying out with our lungs saying thanks to God. We sang our own songs, like OUR GRACE, HALLELUJAH, and more. It was the best day ever. When I was there in the desert singing to God, I've remember about my family and when am I going to ever come out of this book. Everything felt so real, is it just a dream,...I don't really think it is just a dream.

"Are you okay? You look kind of thinkable. Are you okay?" Alex asked me, worried.

"Yeah, I'm....Well, I am kind or sad and happy of something." I said not wanting to make him get more worried.

"Well, don't think that you are going by with it. I know you are worried, and that you are thinking of your family. You have to understand what I am going by and I do understand what you are going through. I hope you understand."

"I do I really do....Lets us to the truth, God almighty." I said begging God.

This is another day with remembrance, happiness and sadness.

Chapter 12

One Year

It had been one year in the book. Sarah was 18 years old and Alex was 19 years old. They were 1 year apart and of course they remember to celebrate their birthday each year, but this is the first time they celebrating birthday.

"Already one year... and still we didn't come out from the book." I said sad.

"It's okay, Sarah. I am that way, too. At least we are together, even if we don't see our family, we have God and together. So if anything happens we will be together to help each other."

"Okay, you always make me happy even if it isn't really real. I thank God that he has send you like someone who really cares about me."

"Well,.... You welcome. Already one year." He said with that sadness and happiness.

"That's what I said......." , "AH<AH<AH<AH!!!" We both laughed.

I wanted him to laugh so we can forget what we talked about it sometimes works, but not always. So we laughed 15 minutes long.

"Wow, you did make me laugh a lot. It feels its was about and hour." Alex said.

"Well, that is awesome. So what are we going to do for, now?" I asked kind of boring. "Don't really know." Alex said mysteriously.

CHAPTER 13
WHO'S THAT?

There was a guy coming along the shore from the pond. I know that you will think that this is going to be kind of weird, but this is how this world is. The guy looked that it was a poor guy. I don't really know how to describe him, but that guy looked a little worried. So, that was the beginning of this guy, I thought.

"Hello, who are you?" Alex asked the guy coming toward us, not saying a single word.

"Hi, who are you?" I asked walking toward him.

Then the guy looked up and said something that we quite couldn't understand.

"What did you say again." We asked together.

Then the guy said it again and this time, we sure couldn't understand.

"Ich habe wirklich Hunger. Kann ich etwas Nahrung haben?" The guy said.

"I think he want some food.....Can you tell that he keeps staring at the food? Poor thing...Please God help us understand...Please?" I said with that faith and then the guy asked me the same thing and this time I understood.

"Ich habe wirklich Hunger. Kann ich etwas Nahrung haben?" The guy asked.

"Oh, sprechen Sie Deutsches. Recht?" I asked.

"Ja tue ich." The guy said.

"Oh, thank you God thank you,...thank you." I said.

"Are you alright? How did you know how to talk to that guy. Man you God has given you how to talk in different languages." Alex said this words as if he never had seen such thing.

"Well, I don't know. I asked God to help me how to talk to that guy and he talks german. The word came out so fast that I didn't know what I said. But then he respond me. That is how I remember what he said he was hungry." I said about crying and Alex hugged me and said, "Don't worry we will give that poor guy something to eat."

I was so happy, so I said, "Wünschen Sie gebratenes Huhn?"

"Bitte ja und danke." The guy was starting to cry.

"Bitte schreien Sie nicht. Was ist falsch?" I asked him to please don't cry. But poor thing that guy was starting crying, I thought.

I gave that guy some fried chicken as I had asked him if he wanted some. After that guy eating, we sure didn't asked his name, because he needed a lot of rest. So we tugged him to sleep, that was a hard work, because he didn't want to stop crying. But this time this day had ended with a guy who needed a lot of hope, love, trustworthy, honesty, and especially love.

"Thank you lord, for letting me talk to that poor guy. For one reason you had let him come to us. We are ready for anything you bring us. Thank you. Amen." I gave a prayer to God for everything. End of the day.

CHAPTER 14

SONDERBAR!!!

It was 5:00 A.M. in the morning and me and Alex woken up to praise the lord, God Almighty. We wash our faces before going under the tree that had good fruits. That tree that had good fruit was a blessing that God had given us. So we go there every morning and give thanks.

This time before waking up I figured out that the guy that came yesterday he was following us. Alex didn't notice that he was, but God gave me that feeling that the guy was following. We started praying to God and started singing some songs that God gave us. Well, that guy needs love and God you had given him the direction to come this way, thank you God, I thought. "Sonderbar"

Then the guy turned around and ran al the way to our tent and where we had our camels, he started crying. I ran after him and said, "Was falsch ist. Sind Sie okay?"

"Mit was befassen Sie sich? Ich bin gut." The guy was confused.

"Ich sah Sie, vollständig zu schreien hier. Ich folgte Ihnen, um zu sehen, wenn Sie gut waren." I said confused, too. I knew he had something wrong.

"Gibt es etwas, das Sie mich von verstecken?" I asked him if he is hiding something from me.

" You don't have to worried of anything. I was just looking for my daughter and you just look like her. That hurt my feelings, that I can't find my daughter." He said with that sadness on his face.

CHAPTER 15
THE TRUTH.

I was kind of worried and I knew that this guy was really sad, and that nothing is going to stop her from knowing the truth.

"Well, then where did you came from Des-Moines, Iowa." He said with that look of lost.

"So how did you come to this place?"

"Well, I was trying to find my daughter,..... Sarah. She looked just like you and she was my only child. I found a book on her bed and I started reading, but before even reading the first sentence I found myself in a war. I was terrified and so I was trying to escape and so I tried, but the soldiers or whatever they were called they hold me back. Then I saw you guys hiding in a blanket. You of sure want to know how I found you. I followed the tracks and then yesterday I found you guys. I haven't eaten since 1 year. God had hold me back and hold my stomach so I wouldn't be hungry. When I talked to you the language I knew that God was going to tell you how to talk, German. That is the way I knew that you were my daughter."

I was so sad, when he finished the last word I was already soaked wet from the crying. "Dad is you.....No,no,no, it can't be....Dad is you. I missed you so much. Please, come, come and hug me so I can feel your warmth and your hug upon me. Please." So he did hugged me and that was how I found my dad. Then Alex came by.

CHAPTER

16 How?

I was so surprised, because Alex went directly to our tent. I saw something was wrong with him. I been with him 1 year and a-almost half. So I told my dad that I will be right back. I went directly to the tent and found him kneel down on his bed and was crying, crying, and crying. I didn't know, of course that what was wrong with him.

"What's wrong, Alex?" I asked trying to calm him down from crying.

"Well,......I am really sad....but really sad, Sarah. I don't really know what to do." He said without stopping the crying he had on him.

"What, what's the problem. Please, tell me. I don't want to be all day worrying about you, that you won't stop crying. Is it because it's time to leave. Did you get hurt?" I was really worried about him. What is wrong with him, I thought.

"No,...no...it's just that I feel sad for my first time,and when I was praying for my family that they could be okay....I just started crying."

"Well, I got good news for you and for me. But I already know what it is. Of course. Do you want to know something interesting?" I said trying to make him smile.

"What,...what is it?" He was kind of smiling and me and I knew this will make him happy, but kind of sad.

"I found my dad, Alex."

"You did? But how. Isn't he outside of the book?" He said confused.

"Yes, he wasssss..... But know he is with us." I said smiling at him.

"Well, where is he?" Alex said with that alert eyes.

"He is outside with the camels....Remember that guy witch one we found?"

"Yeah,....Wait is that him?"

"Yeah, that is him. He is my dad." I said with happiness.

"How did this happen?" He said interested in the story that I was just about to tell.

"Well, why won't you go and ask my dad....He will tell you the whole story."

"Okay, let's go."

We went to see my dad standing there praising God. That is how I think that me and Alex would had praise God, too. We ran toward him and my dad said, "Why do you guys look so interested in me? Did I forget to wash my face and wash my teeth?"

"No, dad,...no." Before I finished my sentence we all started laughing. I haven't laughed so, but so hard in 1 year a-almost a half year. This was the best of the best day ever-Not counting the other best of the best day. But before starting the story Alex, me, and my dad sat on the logs that we had for our fire, then the sun was down. My dad started telling the story and we set the fire up.

We had the best day ever and this was the end of the day...

Chapter 17

WOLVES!!!!!

It was 5:00 A.M. in the morning like always. First we went and wash our faces usually if you want to know the truth we are usually living as the old time zone. My dad's name is Ty, if I didn't say that well know you know what her dad's name is.

We got there about 30 minutes, because Alex kept talking about how we survived the desert and all the time that he wasn't with us-what we did together and more. Finally we got there, first we prayed, then we sand then my dad this time preached the bible. You are wondering about where we got our bibles well, Alex had lived here more and this is the old time zone, so still people had bibles back then. Alex bought some for us.

When my dad was preaching, he was preaching about the demons, that how can the demons get into you. That for me, crept me our a lot. In about 3o minutes there were some wolves hiding on the sand, so no one can see. They were about to start planning something to get their pray, but if you want to know what their pray was, it was.....us. They never made any movements they were like statues. I had never seen this kind of wolves, but al of the sudden I started interrupting the preacher and tell ing him there was a pack of wolves.

Then I saw that same wolf I saw in a long time.

"Alex, there he is that is the same wolf that you told me not to look. Remember?" I asked him frightened.

"Yes, I remember... Ty don't look at that direction..... It's a wolf. The people in this land calls him the DARK DREAMER. If you look back he will follow you where ever you go. That is why he is following, Sarah. Because she looked back in the times that she was frightened."

"I know who he is. He is the biggest demon, he is the chief of the demons of his. I am not afraid with him, because Jesus Christ is my Savior my God, and my Salvation. Go away you pure demons. God doesn't want you here neither do we."

My dad was full with the Holy spirit. If I ever written how that wolf looked like I bet you wouldn't even go on with this book. My dad walked toward it and the wolf walked toward my dad. My dad screamed out loud, "JESUS!!!!" and the wolf exploded with a loud thump and there was dust all over my dad, and again he said, "JESUS!!!" and the dust went flying away inside the sand of the desert.

"Jesus, Jesus,....Jesus is my saviour!!!" My dad kept on singing and screaming the name of Jesus. The other wolves went running as far as they cannot here the name Jesus.

"Wow, you sure is a preacher and you are one of the soldier of God, because I wouldn't not even do that, because I was frightened. You have a big courage and you will be one of those good and best of God preachers."

"Hey, that was totally weird. Remember that we were talking about the demons that how can a demon get into you. Well what you just saw was how you can defeat a demon. Hallelujah, Glory to God who lives!!!"

Chapter 18

Moving.....

We came back to the tent. Alex came and said, "We have to move already. The well is getting out of water and we have to find some place the we can swim and drink water and etc....You get it right? I want to have a good family and your dad needs some where to relax and spend the time with us. What do you think?"

"Okay, then I.....no I mean we will go and talk to him."

"Okay then," Alex was so happy to talk to my dad. They had a good relationship between my dad and him. We went to my dad room or tent and talked to him about the plans, and he really liked it, but he said that we should pray before living and see what God wants us to do and so we did.

"God, please tell us if it is all right to live this place. You know that first we have to pray to you and ask you first than making our own decisions. God help us understand if we don't move we can't be mad at you and if we move it will be the same thing as not moving. Help us please. In the name of Jesus. AMEN!!!" My dad did this prayer and we felt the difference between doing what we want to do than listening to God first. I think it helped a lot.

"Know what do we do?" Alex asked.

"Know we have to wait till God give us the response. I think we will wait till tomorrow." My dad said with that faith that God will.

We waited till tomorrow and waited. It was 5:00 A.M. in the morning and we went to learn about God. My dad again wanted to preach so we let him, because we thought the through my dad God will speak and God did speak through my dad.

My dad was talking about the 10 commandments and we listen very careful. I learned not to tell lies and I started not telling lies, because that is one of the things that God doesn't like. Anyways I never told lies just when I was a little girl. But now I better than tell lies.

Alex learned that you cannot adultery and he usually did some when he was a little kid, but know as I said he knows better than that now. My dad as usual knows all this and so know he is a preacher in Des-Moines. But now he got stuck in this book and now he is preaching to us.

"Dad, don't you miss mom?" I asked after the church was over.

"Yes, I do very much. I hope we will go home pretty soon." Dad said with that sadness, but at the same time he had that same faith look on his face.

We went back to our tent and then we heard a voice calling to my dad.

"Ty I've had heard your prayer. Yes, you may go to a place of how you described it."

"God is that you?"

"Yes, it's me and I tell you that you must go now."

"Yes, God as you say."

Then this was the beginning of packing up our things, Oh my, I thought. We first got our tent packed up and went to the camels to put everything on. But the thing was that we only had 2 camels so we before going on we made a deal. Like always.

My dad and me are riding together and Alex alone, as always. We had that sit for the bump of the camel facing front and so I had to sit on that and my dad on the saddle. At least I was controllable. We were suppose to take turns on the saddle, except Alex he was use to sitting on the saddle.

We got our food on a bag of the old times, but it was cool, because if the food was cold it will stay cold for about 24 hours. That was cool. We got out all the water from the well and put it on a sack of waterproof and we filled it all the way and then the well was empty all empty.

"Time to. Got everything?" My dad said as if he was the boss. It was funny even dad was laughing at his voice and even us, too.

"Yes, sir!" Me and Alex said while laughing.

We got on our camels and headed north. North was cooler because I don't really know. We took a brake and got off on a village that I didn't neither Alex, and neither dad known. They all talk different languages. We still talked on our own language to see if anyone will talk like us.

There was a guy named Williams Smith, who went to us and asked if we were lost.

"No...I don't think so....Well, yeah we are lost." My dad said.

"Okay, then, are trying to go to a river?" Williams Smith asked.

"Yes, we are. Do you know any where that we can find a river around here somewhere?" Alex asked.

"Yes, I know. You guys need a guide? Because I am all open and if anything happens I can help." Williams Smith asked.

"Well, I don't really know......Alex do we need someone?"

"No, I don't think so." Alex said staring at me and thinking about her.

"No, me neither we only need directions." I said.

"Okay, then." My dad said.

Alex came beside me and said, "I don't want no one to take you away from me. I think you are beautiful and I don't want no one trying to take you away from me."

I whispered back to him, "Okay then, if God wants that then we will get together when I am old enough."

"Thanks."Alex was so happy that he kept smiling all the way through our conversation.

"Well, it is okay if you don't need me coming with you guys." Williams Smith kept staring at me and looking at me as if I were his. But thank God Dad, Alex, and me didn't want him to come. Alex kept staring at the guy seriously and the guy didn't like it so he gave us the directions and went to his house with 6 wives out on the street.

"Thank God we didn't let that guy with us." Alex said staring and me and then staring at the guy with 6 wives. The wives looked like sad and looked like they needed help, but they had made a wrong choice only God can help, but I knew if they didn't want to know God they will get stuck in the same place.

"Hey, Sarah, Ty. I had remember about the adultery that you were preaching. Thank you God. Almighty and my Saviour." Alex said with that happiness and faith.

We didn't really don what the guy said where to go. So we tried to find someone that we can trust on. There was a man on the floor hurt. I jumped of the camel and went directly to the guy who was hurt.

"Are you okay? Why are you hurt?" I asked him.

"A whole bunch of guys always hit me and hurt me when I preach to the people and when I even say the word of God, Jesus, and the Holy Spirit." The guy said this words with sadness.

"Oh, I believe in him and my friend and my dad believe on him, too. Do you need a preacher my dad is one. Do you need a hope I am one. Do you need Faith My friend is one. We are all believers in one family. You can join us with our family." I said facing him straight on his eyes. He looked that he had a lot of sadness but at the same time he looked like he will never give up.

"Yes, yes, yes, yes,......Thank you God. Thank you for sending a person to me that will except me." He said it by screaming and crying all at the same time. He looked like those African American that had a lot, but a lot of faith.

"Do you need help to get up?" I asked him, still talking to him.

"Yes, please....Do." He said with happiness.

I went toward my dad and said that this guy needs help, so my dad helped him up and said, "You are welcome, to join our family."

Then Alex went toward the man that was laying down but know that he was standing gave him the hand and said, "You are welcome, and you are welcome to join our family. Any way do you know how to read stars?"

"Yes, I do. I been studying the stars since a little kid. Do you need help on your way to your purpose land?"

"Yes, we do. You know, I don't know how to read stars and if you do we can travel by night time so we can travel."

"Okay, then I will be glad to help you. First, I have to get my camels."

"You said camelsssss?" Alex said impressed.

"Yes I said camels I have 7 seven camels. I have that many, because if someone needs camels than they will get it for free. I am a missionary, and I am a religion of Christian. So, that is what God send me here for. To help the needs."

"Well, Let's go." This was the beginning of the trip with a guy.

CHAPTER 19

THE BEGINNING OF THE TRIAL!!!

We started our trip and it was a lot of fun, because that guy- his name is Margarnexsure- knows a lot about the stars. It was night time but we still went on, we had 3 camels of ourself and 7 camels from Margarnexsure. When I heard his name I thought that he was only kidding. For reals, I thought he was. Then we went to the biggest star in the south so we followed it.

Sometimes we stopped by a well to get some water and to get some rest. By know we should of been there by know, I thought. Because If we didn't stopped we should of been there.

It was the 3rd day traveling and we found traps around the dessert it was afoul there were poor animals that were already dead and that was only laying there and they looked as if there were not even dead. I started crying.

"What wrong, Sarah?" Alex asked.

"Why is it supposed to be so sad and danger in this world? Can't they just have a world of peace and no danger?" I said still crying.

"Sarah, Sarah,,,,, The world it is not only of peace but of danger and war. This years has always been of danger."

I understood, but it is not fair for those poor animals that are dead, they can't pay what the people feel like, it's no fair, I thought. I wanted to tell him that, but it is so hard to, because they won't understand. It was night time again. It had pass the 4th day.

It was morning time and we saw a whole bunch of people coming toward us. It was weird. We stood up watched our faces and said, "Hello, Why are you guys here?"

The people shouted, "We are here to give you this." At the same time they handed over some food new clothing and more valuable things. This was a blessing, we needed food and clothing and more things to survive and get property.

Wait, I thought, they just talked English. I was surprised. We went and thank them and they sang a song, and that for me was a good sign that it was going to be a good day today.

"Let's go you guys and start traveling." My dad said-Ty.

Margarnexsure said, "Are you guys going to eat and then travel or are we going to travel at the same time that we are going to eat?"

I said, "Yeah, that is right we haven't eaten and we are leaving right know."

Ty said, "We are going to eat after we pray and praise God. Remember what I just said that we are leaving means to get ready, Sarah Margarnexsure and Alex. I didn't meant to leave too soon. Come on we better start praying and praising God."

After that talk we started praying and this is how it started the good day. Some times I think that we should pray and praise God and then have my dad- Ty- preach something new. But today we didn't do that, because we have a long day coming on our way.

We prayed and praise God, and right after that Ty started reading a verse and started preaching a little. He said that if we are responsible and do what God says that everything will come out GOOD!!! We went to our place and ate bread, camel meat-that the people just brought us- and fresh fruits. This was delicious, the best food I ever tasted.

I know that it sound weird eating camel meat, but that meat was fresh and that was the only thing that this place ate. Some of the people get lucky if they ate other meat that could be eatable. So, this was just the beginning of the day.

We packed our stuff and we started our journey. This time Margarnexsure let me use one of his camels so I wouldn't be uncontrollable on the back sit, behind my dad. Marganexsure helped me get on the camel, it was fun riding on my own camel- well, yeah. This camel he has given it to me as a gift. We rode, we rode, we rode, we rode. Everywhere we went we were all quite until Margarnexsure said, "Okay, let's start by given the camels some water. They haven't drink water for 5 hours."

"Okay, no problem." My dad said. We got off the camels and we got a bucket of water from the well a mile away and gave the camels a drink.

Chapter 20

An angel.

When we were resting on been on the camels I felt asleep I saw and angel talking to me in my dream. It was a miracle and the angel told me, "Just remember that there is a lot of people out there that are going to try to destroy you future. Listen very carefully Sarah, all the things that are happening to you is to learn how it feel to be in another country and another continent. In 2 months you will be out of this book. When you get out of the book don't do what other people from the world do. Do what God wants you to do. The right thing. Sarah, hear this words and keep it to yourself. Don't say anything yet or the plan of God will be destroyed."

Then after the dream I woken up silently and I was doing what the angel told me to do. My dad, Alex, and Margarnexsure were fixing food so we can travel.

"Sleepy head, you have been sleeping for about an hour. What are you feeling okay, honey." My dad asked me and then something told me to tell him about my dream but I have to pray first.

"I'm okay, dad." I said and then I went and walked away and pray to God, then I heard a voice from the sky.

"My Daughter Sarah, I had heard your prayers and I will tell you the answer. Yes, tell your dad only, he has done what I have said and he will tell you from me what the dream mean. Know stand up." As soon as I stood up there was a tree that was burning with fire and I wasn't scared and I knew that God was with me. I walked back where I was and went to my dad Ty.

"Dad, I want to tell you something."

"What is it, honey."

"I had a dream and I want you to tell me what it means."

I started telling dad about how the angel was and how he told me all this thing, and he said, "Honey, you must have faith, because good things are going to happen in your life. Do what as God tells you and you'll see that he is you guide and your King of Kings and Lord of Lords."

I heard him saying all those words and I felt that I was becoming something else and that everything that is just happening is going to end pretty soon. I was happy for that.

"Wow, do you se that?" Margarnexsure said.

"Yeah, we see it all right." Alex said.

We saw a door, but it wasn't any kind of door it was the biggest door ever it had stairs up, it was going all the way up.

"What could it be?" I asked. I was kind of worry. Well, no the I was always worried about something and then before I can even think I saw a book opened and it was the biggest book ever. So you won't get confused we were all dreaming, but awake dreaming. We went to it and didn't remember that the camels needed food to eat. We climb up and saw the book it had different names on it and then beside that book there was another book and it was not cute or beautiful it was the worst book ever. We sometimes thought that it could be just our imagination, because we were in the dessert, but when all of the sudden we were on our first step for the stairs it felt real. We climb and climb and as I already said there were two books and my dad-Ty- had his bible and he said that it was the prophecy that the book of Revelation said. But just to tell you this is not really is going to happened this is just a book. A made up book. Let's go on with the story. My dad-Ty- read about the prophecy in the book of Revelations.

All of the sudden we came back to where we were feeding the camels and given them some food.

"Dad, I think that I had a dream about a big door and a tall long stairs reaching up in the sky. What does it mean?" I said, wondering about this.

"Sarah, I don't think you are the only one who had dreamed it was just a day dreaming think that I even had that same day dream vision that you had." Ty said- my dad.

"Don't worry, I did get that same dream." Margarnexsure said.

"Me,too." said Alex.

"If we all had that same day dreaming problem, then what does it mean?" I asked.

"I don't really know, but it is just a day dreaming we should ask God about this." My dad said.

My dad is alway talking with faith and never saying let forget it. I like my dad, that is what I like about him. Sometimes he is hard to handle, but he is nice and when he is like that he. Well, I just think that he has changed since he gotten here with us.

We went back to the other subject we had, about how are we going to go there. But when they were talking about that I was just focusing of the day dreaming I had and the others had.

We got on the camels each of us and started our journey. We were are close to where we want to go. It was a very tired day and tomorrow is my birthday and I wanted to wish we go back home to find my mom and hug her and have my life with my parents. I wanted to be a missionary when I go back to my world. I don't really want to think of my back life. Every time my parents had fight was all because of me and know and then I won't make my parents fight, I thought this words on my mind and I was really happy of what I thought. This is why all this was happening to me. I was a bad girl back then, and know I had changed. That is what God wanted me to do.

"Are you okay, honey?" My dad asked-Ty.

"Yes, dad I am just so happy of what had just happened to me all these years, sorry dad. For being mean to you back then. Will you forgive me?" "Yes, Honey. I will."

Me and my dad started crying and me and my dad were all doing this blooper. Alex and Margarnexsure were staring at us, but when I saw them they were trying to hold there tears back and it was an incredible time.

CHAPTER 21
FOUND THE PLACE.....

We had found the place we were looking for and while we were still getting to that place my dad was crying and singing songs that I never heard. The song that my dad was singing. I think it was German song, because I joined in with him and it was usually fun. After I had joined in I was seen that I wasn't the only one singing, that Margarnexsure and Alex were singing, too.

We put our tent up on the place, the best place we could found in the land that it was already ours. Sometimes I thought that this will never happen, but we made it and here we are praising God for what he has done for us. That was the most beautiful land I had ever seen. That is what God has given us.

I found in pond a lot of fishes and they looked beautiful. I went to my dad and asked, "Dad, is it okay if I can go and swim with the fishes?"

"Yes, honey. Go and go swim with the fishes." My dad eyes looked really happy, the happiest smile and eyes that I had never seen. I went where Alex was and I said, "How do you do?"

"Oh, well tired and just tired and sweaty."

"Do you want to go and swim with me and play?" I asked with the biggest smile I ever had, I knew he will say yes. So I said, "See you there. I am going to be waiting for you and if Margarnexsure will like to come then I'll see him, too." I said facing to Margarnexsure who was happy to go with us.

I went to dad and asked, "Do you want to come and swim with Alex and Margarnexsure?"

"No, honey, I have to go and see what is more out there. I will be to that North side mountain and be praying. Honey, please do not disturb me, I will be praying." My dad said starting walking toward that mountain side. As soon as he was far away, I said, "See you at supper time dad.....LOVE YOU!!!" He waved see ya wave and I did too.

I went to the pond and there they were already swimming without letting me know. I took the heavy clothes off and I had my shorts and my t-shirt on to go swim. All of the sudden they push me in the pond and we started splashing water to each other.

"Hey, Sarah." Alex said at the middle of the pond.

"Come here I want to show you something."

I went swimming toward him and he said, "Lay on your back and float on the water then look above you and tell me what you see and what you feel."

I did as what he has told me and I laid on the water floating and letting all my body do what ever it want to do. I closed my eyes and I felt peaceful and when I looked above me as what Alex told me I saw that I was flying in the air.

"Oh,...Oh,..... I feel I'm flying Alex. Join me and we both will float together." I said. Alex did what I told him and so he was floating beside me and we were holding hands as if we were birds flying up and not knowing that it felt as we were in this land.

"You know what I think? I think that pretty soon we will go home......pretty soon." Alex said with the peacefulness voice that I never heard before.

I closed my eyes and smelled the peacefulness air and feel free. That is how I feel. I felt like something was holding me and that I will never be alone. With Alex, Margarnexsure, Ty-dad-, and God. I will never be alone even if there aren't there we will always be together by heart. Even my other family that aren't here was with us.

Chapter 22

My dwelling place should be....

When we got done with swimming I prepared the supper before my dad came. I prepare Chicken Fushi. That is how this world calls it. So I don't know why, I asked Margarnexsure but he doesn't really know. But still I went on cooking supper. Then all of the sudden I started reading the bible until the food was ready I read that my dwelling place should be Jesus. That was cool and interesting for me. I went on with the reading and Dad just came in the tent and saw me reading.

"Is the food, ready, honey?" Dad said tired.

"Yes, dad it is almost ready here it this so you can wait for at least 5 minutes of hunger."

"Thank you honey I will go and get the boys."

"Sure dad go ahead." I said still interested on this verses. I went on reading until about 10 minutes they came so I started putting some food on the plates and did the table for them. It wasn't only Chicken Fushi, there was corn, bread, rice, and Bohnen (beans). Bohnen means as you can see beans, Bohnen is a German word for beans.

We ate and talked for a long time then my dad came up with a good idea build some houses our time house made out of wood and live there as long as God want us to live. This was the day of the first day on the beautiful land.

Chapter 23
Five Years later.....

Five years had passed and me and Alex got married in that same place where we were trying to find our land. Before getting married we already did our houses and started having our plummeting attached the houses. But know Alex and me were married and we weren't going to plan having baby. God is the one who says when and where. I learned it in the bible.

I wish we were back to our home our real home where there is cars and you know what else. Anyway in this period of times I was teaching myself of how I should be a teacher. I always wanted to be a teacher and know look I'm here stuck still in this book somewhere that may be my mom can't find.

After the marriage I went to my own house without paying any bills that was one of the things I liked the old days, because you didn't have to pay bills. I was at my house picking up the mess that the guys always make trying to fix the plummeting. Anyway it felt as if the first day that we found this land, well it felt as if the day are going really fast I just can't wait to go back to out normal lives.

CHAPTER 24

GOING HOME.....

I found this book laying on the dirt and when I saw it, it was the same one that I had when I was in the library. We might go home with this, I thought. I went to Alex- who was know my husband and he was loyal and handsome he was my friend but know he is my guy who will always worry about me- show him the book and he was crying he said, """"I had a dream, Sarah. That we were going home and that we will be missionaries but before that we were in college to study for what God wanted us to be when we grow up. So you found that same book. I am so happy!!!! Thank you Lord."""""

I hugged him and we both were crying and happy that we were going back home. We both went to my dad and to Margarnexsure. I knew that I was going to miss Margarnexsure because he was one of those in the book, I think so. They were all happy even Margarnexsure that was crying and at the same time he said, "I'm going home thank you lord."

"So you are saying that you are not from here?" My dad asked him.

"No, sir....I'm not from here. I am the arthur from the book you are in right know. I am a writer and then God had send me in here to see what I had written and to tell the world that living in this life isn't fun and that this book will help missionaries to know how it is living in this place like this." Margarnexsure said at the same time crying.

"Wow, so God has send us in this book to know how it feels to be a missionary and how know and days it is way different but there is still places like this." Alex said.

"So how are we going to find to go home know?" I asked.

"What does God want us to do before going on with our life?" Margarnexsure asked back.

"PRAYYYYYYYYYYYYYYY!!!!!!!!!!!!!!!" Dad said with happiness. We took 4 days without eating and prayed and prayed and never stopped until we saw an angel standing with a door beside it. Yes, going home....going our sweet home. Before going the angel said, "To those who want to go home pass this door and to those who don't stay."

We didn't hurry to the door we were taking time to pray again to the lord, our God. For thanks. We all hold our hands and pass through the door and with our face crying we were happy to go home back to those who needs the word of God. That will be missionaries.